Poetic Relationship Moments

Michael G. Wright

Copyright © 2024 Michael G. Wright
All rights reserved
First Edition

Fulton Books
Meadville, PA

Published by Fulton Books 2024

ISBN 979-8-88982-816-7 (paperback)
ISBN 979-8-88982-817-4 (digital)

Printed in the United States of America

Acknowledgment

Thanks, Mom, for being my guardian angel! I wouldn't have survived without you. I love you. ♥

First Date

Ready for a perfect date with a beautiful lady who has great taste. We can start with wine and cuddle most of the time. Then eat lots of food that gives us pleasure. Damn, what a treasure. We'll enjoy the stars shining so bright, makes us want to never say good night. With roses ready to bloom and nothing stopping us from going home too soon, you keep putting me in this good mood, hope I don't sound too rude. I'm excited that I don't have to focus on myself since I keep thinking of someone else. Glad to be hanging out with the best, wouldn't expect any less.

Bad Memory

I remember a date that started with hate. Although it was the beginning, I prepared for the end, knew your heart would never bend. I'm not a psychic in any way, but my soul is counting down to doomsday. As I picked you up for a stroll, I pretended love was our goal. I hoped my heart would cope; please don't make me heaven's next joke. It's so ridiculous that I fell for your reflection; now my heart is in witness protection. Our last day came and brought shame; sorry your heart never knew my name.

Color-Blind

Color shouldn't matter in this equation; it's about human relations. Loved you from first sight, getting to know you was more than right. I was afraid to show my emotions, thought I would drown in your ocean. We are so strong together, looking like two birds wearing the same feathers. Throwing your hate at us just increases our trust. Anybody doubting our existence will be overwhelmed by our persistence. We have a goal of our own, neither of us will end up alone. Calling us names won't bring shame to our game. We've survived worst; our love won't fit in a hearse. Of course, we'll love each other tomorrow, not going to face any sorrow. Our complexions won't hold us back; God is our witness, and that's a fact. Our skins are not the same; however, it's more important to share a last name. My heart will eventually expire, but our love won't retire. My feelings for you are beyond what is true. We have been through thick and thin; at the end, we always win. This is not easy to keep together, harder than predicting weather. Sometimes we need our separate space to help us reach a better place. Not so easy to follow that advice; God and you told me twice. Pleasing everyone is not the way; we need love to get us through another day. Again, we will laugh about what others say since I am your night and you're my day. Those who never try won't ever see past their eyes.

Undercover Trouble

She doesn't want us to be hand in hand; her focus is a more devious plan. Trying to seduce me at every turn, she's hoping to make my heart burn. She has no chance in this endeavor, better luck predicting the weather. I'm your man, and I know my worth; I've loved you since birth. This is not the end of our story; your best friend wants to steal our glory. She moves like a thief in the night, that's why no man can endure her sight. Always wanting what others possess, she's cursed to be stuck at second best. Changing her won't be simple; it's not like erasing a pimple. No matter what happens, stick close to me, we still have the same destiny.

Never Enough

Your mother treats me like a lamb; apparently, she doesn't know who I am. She believes I'm her competition, time to start my petition. I should be first in your life, the one you call wife. Your mom cooks and cleans, but I work and stay lean. Always putting up with her words of hate while we share a dinner plate. Didn't sign up for an execution; this is against the constitution. Nowhere else to go, time to say goodbye to this puppet show. Expressing my emotions should show I'm deeper than any ocean. Last chance to change our fate, your mother still wishes we never went on a date.

Never Again

Brushing my teeth never hurt so much until your touch. Punching me in the face for no reason then say you're teasing. That was dead wrong, treated me like King Kong. Always craving your attention, but this I can't mention. Normal people don't act like this; I'm beyond pissed. With a black eye and a swollen lip, I should exit this *Titanic* ship. Love may have been our boarding pass, but there's not enough gas to last. Every day I get a scar; my soul forgot who you are. Beating on me brings you pleasure, rather you treat me like King Tut's treasure. Give me credit for not fighting back; I'm showing you where the love is at. Never thought a woman would hurt me like this and give me a kiss. Although I'm big and strong, I allowed you to treat me wrong. If we continue on this path, someone may retire beneath the grass.

No Shame

If I stopped by, would I see a lie in your eye? What is that scent I smell? Is it a sign of you breaking out of your shell? Something feels wrong as I travel through these doors, someone else has taken what's yours. I'm not the first and probably not the last; soon she will be stuck in my past. I should have seen the signs, this wasn't my time. No more doubts, please get out. How can I still care when you refuse to share? Mistakes were made on both sides, but now there's nowhere to hide. Making a confession to my face won't bring us back to a good place. More time must pass so my heart doesn't feel last. If I left, it might be for the best. Not sure about the answer, but you ripped through me like cancer.

Last Dance

With roses in hand and candles lit, I knew we would be a great fit. You've been legendary from the start, can't imagine us apart. Unfortunately, when I walked in, I was blindsided by an unforgivable sin. Never thought this would happen in my life, wasn't ready to dump my wife. Screams echoing in the hall, knew it wasn't from a fall. Hoped it was a mistake; however, my heart continued to break. As I entered our room, nothing was left to assume. She stared and didn't care. They had a blast and put me in the past. Those bedsheets forgot my name; now I've been forced out of the game.

Beautiful

I'm not sure where to start, but you should know you're my heart. Seeing you for the first time blew more than just my mind. Those deep eyes and warm smile make me feel like the luckiest guy. While sleeping throughout the nights, I wondered if I'd wake up to see your beautiful sight. Although that's a dream that has come true, nothing else makes me feel closer to you. Getting to know you has been my pleasure, can't be matched by any treasure. Loving you is a dangerous thing, causes me to be vulnerable within. However, I'm willing to take that chance; you're worth every bit of this romance. Thanks to you, I don't have to settle for less; now I'm hanging with the best. You're as fine as wine with so much desire, makes me want to jump into your fire. I can't contain this endless fire; I want you to feel my passion and desire. No way out of this hot kitchen; you have my soul constantly itching. Your beauty can't be stopped; it will take you to the top. The look in my eyes will sting you at first, but you'll end up sharing my thirst.

Beauty and the Least

See me in the mirror, and you may think twice then realize I'm just as nice. Sorry I'm not pretty like the angels at church, but I have a soul that can get hurt. Can't fight fate, I was born into hate. If my exterior matched the interior, I would be superior. Worshipping you like the sun as you stare at me like I'm dumb. Tired of hiding in the car while you're enjoying the bar. I sound so pathetic, wish I was athletic. Swore I had a plan but still not your man. Although I wish I shared your beauty, this should be another man's duty.

Before Next

When I'm near, how do you feel? Is it something you try to conceal? Does running into me every day turn your heart away? Knowing how close I am to you leaves my heart without a clue. When you hear my name, do you still feel the same? As you stare at me, what do you see? If I was gone and you were here, would you think of me through your tears? Does your heart stand still when I'm away? Is it a waste to ask anyway? When did my touch stop feeling like much? Just when I thought I've seen it all, I realized you let me fall. You never let me know; you had the urge to go. Should I seek another path and leave you alone at last? Will it brighten your day to know I've moved on, that my tenderness for you has gone?

Can't Wait

My heart skips a beat whenever I hear your feet. It's a natural feeling to see you're so appealing. When you say hi, my heart turns shy. Seeing you shouldn't hit me so hard, but you make me drop my guard. It's an impossible task to pretend we won't last. You are special in every way; I swear you're better than any holiday. You got my mind stuck in time, feeling like I'm drinking wine. If you have a question, I'll have the answer; I want to be your private dancer. Honey, you're as smooth as glass, don't ever want to be your past. Tell me how to make you mine, don't stop if I cross the line. So hard to resist you in every way, that's why I asked God for another day. With you, I could never be out of luck since you're my million bucks.

Check Me Out

Before you stop by, call me first; I want to make sure to wear a nice shirt. Looking good for you is priority, not trying to date a sorority. Wanting to impress you like when we met, showing the world who is the best. You are righteous in every way; God couldn't create you in one day. Since you're beyond beauty and style, my heart will stay warm for a while. Words alone can't describe my luck; breathing without you would suck. You are the master of my fate; God and I know you can make my heart break. Because you know my truth more than any other, I must trust you like my mother.

Christmas Love

To the warmest heart I have ever met, I want to wish you Christmas's best! Hope all your wishes come true because you deserve it too. Like an angel in the sky, you hold yourself up very high. Nothing ever holds you back, and that's a trait most people lack. Follow your heart in the right direction and come close to perfection. A new year is coming around; hopefully we are still heaven-bound. If Santa forgot to stop by your house last night, God will still be your guiding light. However, after sliding down your chimney, I'd leave you a gift; yes, it would give your heart a lift. You're sweet as sugar and smooth as ice; you make me feel beyond right. Starting with a stare, then a smile, followed by a wink which will make your soul sink. Stronger than day and night, your faith shines eternally bright. You have been great all year long; now you've earned my heart's song.

First

Before giving you my greatest possession, I should start with a simple confession. I'm scared to trust, don't want this to be lust. Didn't think you would say yes so quick thought it was a trick. This is the beginning, and I feel like singing. Finding a comfortable place is the key, then it's you and me. Nonetheless, I'm supposed to wait for marriage and a baby carriage. Breaking a vow to make you happy now. This is my first time crossing the line. Please be gentle; this is going to be monumental. Promise you'll stay all night and hold me tight. I shouldn't regret what can't be reset. It's not a burden to be a virgin.

I Wish

Today at the wishing well, there was a dream I needed to tell. Holding you close throughout the night makes my heart shine so bright. Seeing your beauty inside and out shows me what life is supposed to be about. Your hand in mine in the dark, never straying too far apart. Touching my soul every hour, scared about giving you all that power. Getting to know you day by day, hoping to impress you in every way. You should know my true intention; it starts and ends with keeping your attention. With God and you by my side, there's no reason for me to hide. Looking forward to next time, just make sure I stay at the head of the line.

Just Once

As I woke, I hoped fate didn't make me a joke. We were lying in bed, but nothing was said. Thought it was my fault for accessing your vault. Was this a onetime thing, or does it end with a ring? Would you be sad if this created someone who calls me Dad? Would our parents agree with us being so free? Furthermore, your friends may struggle with this issue and need a tissue. Not sure what to think; you jumped me before I blinked. No reason for us to play shy; we're not ready to say goodbye. Sounds like a simple solution may turn into a prosecution. There's no right or wrong, just a question of how long.

Long Distance

What did you mean when you hung up? Was it true when you said our love is out of luck? I thought this was just another fight, not enough for you to leave on a flight. Talking to you on the phone every day doesn't make us okay. The deep connection is there, but I need you here. Think about this, you are my first and last wish. Longing for better times, praying that you're more than lines. Protecting my heart from going insane, hoping you and God treat me the same. Got to be real about what's said and done because I'm the earth and you're my sun. I've been leaning on your words, begging to be heard. Slowing down around every turn, feeling like I'm about to get burned. Don't know where to go from here, give me a reason not to disappear.

Messed Up

Waking up alone doesn't feel right, can't remember what happened last night. This is not a medical condition, more like an addiction. Drinking and driving don't mix, a devastating issue to fix. Drugs combined with drinking is another disaster that will deliver me to the hereafter. Upsetting loved ones for no reason, continuing to torture everyone despite the season. Checking into rehab may be the answer, got to fight hard like battling cancer. My partner and children need me longer, together we grow stronger.

More than a Dream

This is more than I imagined, you can clearly see; I'm soaring on the wings of infinity. Hoping it's more than biology, praying for an "A" in chemistry. Lost in a sea of endless emotions, seeking a cure for this love potion. Let me reveal my true intention; this rises above any perfection. Don't fear my wrath, just be part of my dreams, awake my soul, and read what it means. To beat as two hearts but breathe as one, that's the feeling which can't compare to none. Without your sweet touch, the game called life doesn't mean that much. You're so much fun; I'm like the earth and you are my sun. Baby, you're on my mind 24-7; are you sure you didn't fall from heaven? In my heart and life, you're the only beauty I call Mrs. Wright.

More than You

What is the secret of success? Why does love keep making me second-best? How do I pursue a ring when no one wants to let my heart in? Love, do you hear my plea? Why am I always left behind to bleed? Please let me know when it's time to join the show. Hand in hand and cheek to cheek is what everyone seeks. Once again, I'm called a friend; this only leads to a dead end. Tired of this fate, my heart shouldn't have to wait. How do I become one of those guys who never have to try and lie? Give me a second glance so I can put you in a trance. People want you wherever you go; you don't know about feeling low. Don't want attention from any other, just stop treating me like your brother. I would love to hear you cheer and sometimes call me dear. Want you to see me as a man, don't confuse me with a lamb. Trust me, I'm as good as it gets; don't worry about losing that bet. With this confession, I'll teach you a lesson. I always knew I was good enough although you made me feel like I never mattered much. This is a needle in my eye which would make any man cry. I want to stand tall, not keep hiding behind walls. When you look at me, you don't crave what you see. Yes, I must agree that you are not for me. I'm a knight in shining armor, stop treating me like a pig farmer. Pay attention to this letter; I just proved God made me better. You can never hurt me again; life made me a perfect ten.

No Title

You know what's lame? You're afraid to say my name. Always hoping no one will know so I won't spoil your show. I'm always in disguise, no need for you to hide. Embarrassed by my wit and charm, you secretly wish me harm. You want everyone to believe we're just friends; that's where this fairy tale ends. Being happy and hopeful is what I want to know, but you keep giving me reasons to go. I'm worth the time as any other, so please stop treating me like your brother. No need for an apology or expensive things, just tell me when the love begins. Still waiting in line for your love to make my heart shine.

No Trust

You asked me if I'm single, and I have proven my worth; now help me break this curse. Bring me to your house so I can erase all doubt. Need to see if you sleep alone, can't tell that over the phone. I want to close my eyes and not lose any rest, constantly wondering who you like best. It's hard when trust is a must. For us to keep this right, I will have to follow you every night. This may seem weird at first, but I can't stop and reverse. Losing you now would be a threat to what makes my heart work best. Please understand this prediction; my feelings for you are more than an addiction. Never had anyone like you, holding my heart together like Krazy Glue. I'm still learning how to defeat deception and transform it into a wedding reception.

No Pressure

Finally feeling human again, now I can call you a friend. Been a long time since I could breathe and not have to hear you plead. Thank you for calming my mind and helping my heart unwind. Not your fault for trying so hard; you really helped me to drop my guard. The damage was done before you stepped into my life; sorry I wasn't looking for a wife. Your kindness was a wonderful thing but not deserving of a ring. Hate me if you must, I never betrayed your trust. I'm so grateful to be free, without love leaning on me.

Obsessed

What made you love me first? What caused you to feel the thirst? Was it the way I held your hand and made your heart soar like Peter Pan? Only I can make you shout without words coming out. Giving you so much guilty pleasure, convincing you to share your most precious treasure. This was so good, but then you hunted me like Robin Hood. No space for myself, had to call 911 for help. Needed some time alone so I could find my way home. Not easy to step away and see you around the corner another day. There's no way to correct this mess; God and I tried our best. For the future, follow this advice; it takes more than a pretty face to become a wife.

Over

Did gaining weight cause this hate? She gave me a baby, but all I see is her eating gravy. Remembering when you were light as air, now you feel like a polar bear. Meanwhile, my love handles are hard to hide; they require a tour guide. Tired of holding my stomach in, God and Mom would say that's a sin. We became too comfortable with each other; we almost look like brothers. It's time to change things around, no more lying on the ground. Couples should do better than this, don't slip into our senseless abyss.

Not Again

What I saw couldn't be real; you told me how you feel. That smile, that face, this must be a mistake; your love could never be fake. Say it isn't so, another love filling me with whoa. What was once in your heart has disappeared and been replaced with tears. I should've seen the signs and read between those lines. Every word you spoke was nothing but a joke. How is it that I usually choose wrong? Why does it always end like a sad love song? Taking chances is part of the game, but I'll never trust the same. Despite adversity, I will survive even though I'll continue drying my eyes. Next time I'll try harder, which is no guarantee; I know love is waiting for me. Patience is a virtue I must learn to prevent me from getting burned.

Shadow

In the shadows, I hide while feeling so empty inside. Claiming you love me with every breath, but your heart still won't say yes. Every day I call and hear your voice, so why not make me your love choice? Torturing me by watching you hold his hand drowns my heart in quicksand. Sneaking around to keep your affection is not what I call perfection. He gets vacations and dates; however, you ask my heart to wait. Not fair for you to keep picking another since I love you like no other. Because we're lovers and best friends, no way this dream should end. Life without me hurts; don't want your heart to burst. Don't abuse me because of the past; we own a love that will last.

Second Best

Blinded by your beauty and grace, I thought this was the right place. As you entered the room, my heart was doomed. Catching your attention with my words and charm, never expected any harm. Trying to impress you with luxurious things made my heart sing. I write letters and call, so why is your heart an unbreakable wall? What makes him more perfect than me? My heart beats twice as fast for thee. He hurts you from head to toe while my love continues to grow. Promising to treat me the same, convinced me I was in the game. Nevertheless, you forgot my name; what a shame. That's not fair; I deserve better, hopefully you respond to this poetic love letter.

Perfection

You stop me and drop me in every direction; it's beyond any affection. Your sophistication is unmatched; you are the sweetest catch. With perfection untold, your beauty can cure the common cold. I want to impress what God already made the best. I'm searching deep in my heart to find where the fire starts. Just open your eyes to a new direction; yeah, it's us, a better perfection. When you stare at my heart, it hits me like a dart. Don't be shocked that you have my heart locked. Your beauty is as pleasant to me as honey is to a bee. Seeing you every night convinces me that God was right.

So Sorry

I treated you wrong for so long. Should have showered you with kisses and called you Mrs. You were supposed to be my queen; instead, I introduced you to mean. You were right from first sight. How can I make it up to you? Only God and you know what to do. Forgive me for being a fool although I should have figured out what to do. Never want you to feel sorrow; I'll always love you tomorrow. What can I do to erase our bad past and show how our love lasts? All truth, no lies, I appreciate what's behind those beautiful eyes. I couldn't ask for a better friend and lover; my heart wouldn't accept any another.

After You

Hello to a familiar friend who I usually meet at the end. Being alone gives me time to think so I won't easily fall for the next wink. You know my name and circumstance; all I fear is another romance. Make me hate my heart so I won't fall apart. Keep my thoughts away so love will not come this day. To hear my voice and no other relieves my soul so love doesn't bother. Wanting more shouldn't be a curse, just trying to keep my heart out of a hearse. With all this pain, how do I stop becoming insane? Not easy to endure this stress, been expecting the very best. Staying alone may be my fate, but my heart hopes it's not too late.

Our Valentine's Day

I can't say everything in one day, pray our love will show me the way. Thanks for teaching me how to trust; learning love is beyond a crush. Taking my hand and guiding me gently, treating me like a new Bentley. Keep reminding me of what it took to get your second look. It wasn't easy for you and me; sometimes it felt like I died. We just need to cuddle to keep our love out of trouble. It doesn't take much to feel that love rush. When we grow older and remember this day, what will your heart say? We deserve a love that's true, starts with me and ends with you. Smiling each day as I rise, seeing endless love in those eyes. Love me for me, I won't let you down; end of the day, you'll be wearing my crown. You're the queen of my heart and all I desire; everything about you ignites my fire. My feelings for you will never waver; please keep love in our favor.

One More Time

I'm learning to forgive, but I'll never forget; our future is not all set. Still hurts to say your name, wish someone else would wear that shame. You were the love of my life, the one whom God made me love twice. In my dream, you're awake, asking me for another date. Look into my eyes and you will see no lies. What does it take to put your mind at ease? How many ways can I say *please*? My thoughts are as real as my touch; stop thinking I don't love you so much. This is the last time I'll bow, so hear my vow. I need you to give me life by becoming my wife.

The One

Since I spoke your name, my heart hasn't been the same. First I was blinded by your amazing eyes, followed by no damn lies. Didn't know something was missing until you made my heart stop and listen. If beauty was a game, everyone would be screaming your name. Being sexy, classy, and cool seems to come natural to you. Getting to know you is an unexpected treat, which no amount of money can beat. Not what I planned, instead what I found, is that I want to keep your heart around. It's not difficult to put these words together, hoping for a beautiful endeavor. It would be awesome to talk until the sun goes down, then I would take you all over town. Without hesitation, I would try my best, don't expect any less. Give me a chance to show you perfection; it's not hard, just stare at your reflection.

Unforgettable

I'll always be in love with that smile and enjoy holding your hand for a while. You make my heart shake like a first date. Those eyes are amazing to me; you look hotter than a hundred degrees. I want to have a great life with a woman that is hotter than any wife. *Love* is a word that people say, but I want you to know you really make my day. With eyes like diamonds and lips so sweet, of course, I want you as my treat. You're sexy from head to toe, love you when you come and go. Don't ever leave for too long; my heart will always keep singing your sweet song. I drown in the moment when it comes to you, that's what love will do. Those eyes tear me up, feeling like a new pup. Without warning, you knocked me on the ground; now I have to yell your name around town. This feeling can never go away; thank God for making you my Christmas Day.

This Time

It's back again, another chance, hopefully to figure out the word *romance*. Easy to say, hard to do; if you don't watch out, you'll look like a fool. If I'm smart, I will learn from the past, so this time, my heart won't end up in a cast. This time, before I tell her my name, I'll let her know I'm not playing games. What I need from her is love and admiration, not to be a figment of my imagination. I should have enough faith to tell you anything, also be able to treat you like a diamond ring. When you ask me how I feel, my words should not faze you; I thank God every day for making you.

Wild Thing

Years have gone by, but I still try. Surprising you at every turn sometimes gives me heartburn. I'm trying to keep you guessing without undressing. Wanting to spice things up and make you feel like your soul will erupt. Got ideas that will blow your mind and make your body unwind. Need to keep you off track so you'll know where the love is at. I may confuse you a little because it sounds like a riddle. This will teach you to appreciate my style and follow me for a while. I'm better than Superman in every way; I'll swoop down and save your day. I still got what it takes to make your heart shake. Need to remind you where I'm from; I'm the guy who you should have brought to the prom. You're still the same woman that's so right; God would definitely make you twice.

Without You

This is my life, a man without a wife! This journey began in the past and almost made me last. Of course, I knew better but still did anything to get her. Followed my heart without pause, gave destiny a cause. The future knows my name, no way will my heart be the same. Tried to learn from the past, however, ended up feeling like an ass. As time went on, I prayed for better. Why is my soul a little deader? Talking only goes so far, just confess who you are. Is this a blessing in disguise or a soul that wasn't wise? Should I have slowed down instead of running through town? The time has come for me to stop feeling numb. I want more, don't want to be a bore, show me how to be adored. What must I do to change my fate? How do I tell heaven I can't wait? These are the thoughts that shake my mind while others sit and unwind. For me to be like the rest, I have to accept that God knows best. Show me how to get on love's list; it costs no more than a simple kiss.

Worthless

I dealt with the ex who never let me rest. Apparently, I enjoyed the abuse despite my heart yearning for a truce. You hurt me unlike no one before, danced on my heart like it was a hardwood floor. Without hesitation, you broke my wall, left me hanging like a waterfall. Why did you treat me this way? Why was my name so hard to say? I just wanted simple dinners; instead, you reminded me I wasn't a winner. You put me down and turned my soul into a clown. No one wants to exist like this, feeling as though I'm not worthy of a kiss. I died again and still no end. You've broken my joy, played with my heart like a toy. One day I'll forget this hurt and finally prove my worth.

Not Now

Years from now, be ready for me; I want to make our family. We'll love our children and meet new friends; life together won't ever end. Enjoying simple moments like staring at a star, proud to know who you are. Dancing on air as we grow older, realizing our bond which gets bolder. Although the adventure hasn't begun, you will be the one. Soon you'll see you mean more to me than eternity. I will kiss and caress then keep showing you my best. Look into my heart and see, I'm also known as destiny. Showing I care with a simple look, you should be able to read me like a book. I want you from head to toe; I can never let you go. You're more than meets the eye; you give me strength to try. Love knows your name; that's why God made our hearts the same. You make me crazy without trying; that's why my heart keeps crying.

The Proposal

How do I show I'll never let you go? I'm down on one knee without hesitation, hoping you won't change before my presentation. Passing you the key to my heart may not be so smart. Reaching for your hand means more to me than a hundred grand. No limit to how this will be done, but it shouldn't make your heart run. This needs to be a surprise that will erase all lies. Where can I take you to perform this deed and not cause my heart to bleed? Hope it happens under the moonlight; what an unforgettable sight. We would be on the beach at last, saying goodbye to the past. I'm ready to make this work; please, love, don't hurt. I ask you with my heart in hand, make me happier than Disneyland.

Bachelor Party

Tonight I may get naughty, but I'll remember to act like I'm forty. Going to have fun with the guys; however, nothing to make you dry your eyes. We'll have some drinks, not enough to end up in a sink. I want to check out some dancing and practice a little romancing. I'll throw some dollars around and pretend not to make a sound. I may tell them a lie or two, but no one can equal you. Just hanging with my friends, hoping this night will never end. This type of fun can never be overdone. Looking forward to running through town while keeping my eye on the final countdown. Although I'll be enjoying the sights, glad to know I'm going home to Mrs. Wright. Thank you, wife, for this treat; that's why you're my only sweet.

Last Fling

Before we wed, do you want to wake up in another person's bed? Have you earned the right to tell another person good night? These are the questions that roam my mind, trying to avoid staying blind. Trusting you to have the time of your life but still awake as my wife. You deserve this as much as any another; however, don't forget you're a mother. When you're passionate with him, remember he's just a guy with limbs. While I slept, you believed I was deaf. This is the reason my heart calls you treason. I should be roaming in your mind at night, but you keep wishing to see another sight. You need something to turn you on, but somehow that would make me gone. Admit it, you think I'm not real even though most consider me a steal. Treat me like the president, instead of a mere resident. Why do you keep searching for more, pretending I'm an eyesore? Explain to me how I let you down, especially after I bought you a wedding gown. There's no way I can be perfect, but don't think I'm your circus. This man is not equal to me; he can't make you smile from sea to sea. Please stop looking for better; damn it, I'm your love letter.

Showtime

When we wed, our hearts will be fed. Staring down the aisle, feeling like a newborn child. Our guests are loving your dress; you bring new meaning to the word "impress." You looked so good coming from that limo truck, think I heard God say, "Good luck." Today, everyone wants to be you; too bad there's only room for two. With my tuxedo too tight and your gown so right, we are making history tonight. Now we're standing in front of the preacher, feeling our love growing deeper. We created this dance that evolved into an endless romance. As we say yes, our souls will confess. This is our time when love flows like a nursery rhyme. Let's seal this deal with a kiss and thank God for granting our only wish.

Firstborn

Been almost a year, you're about to see my tears. You've been baking in your mom for a while, time to meet you with a smile. I'm going to be a dad, never again will my heart turn sad. When you come out, heaven will shout. With those little tears so golden and my love for you unfolding, our beautiful eyes match; that's where the love is at. With skin as amazing as mine, of course, our love will shine. Be the reason I don't lie when I say you come from God's eye. Never trade you for anything; you are my angel wings. I'll always show you I care since you mean more to me than air.

Unequal

You make more money than me; that's not how it's supposed to be. I'm the provider, not an outsider. I want you to be a success, but I shouldn't feel like I'm wearing your dress. I'll feed the family and keep us out of debt; don't count me out yet. Understanding our struggle prepares me for any trouble. Every king needs a queen; you'll always be seen. Need your support, just don't make me feel like I'm in court. Fortunately, you're educated and have style; I've depended on my muscles for a while. Competing with you is not my intention; instead, I'm praying for redemption. A wallet doesn't define my worth; it's a lesson I learned from birth. Thank you for carrying the load, time for me to take over the road.

Temptation

If I look at you, my feelings will shine through. You make me nervous in every way; you make love seem okay. I respect you with all my heart, so I pray we won't start. Seeing you throughout the day makes my heart betray. So hard to hide my affection since I yearn for this love connection. It's hard to know your thoughts; I understand love can't be bought. You brighten the sun with that smile; you stopped my heart for a while. I need to forget your face so we can avoid first base. Touching you at any time should be more than a crime. You make me roar, and that scares my mind, no room for me to unwind. Being next to you can't be the plan; it's not as easy as getting a tan. Of course, I can change my life but don't want to lose my wife.

Older and Bolder

Gray hair has come our way; we know it plans to stay. Aches are now the norm, but we learned to conform. However, we still find time to sit and drink wine. Although we may not be able to walk fast, this love definitely lasts. Hearing your voice is such a pleasure; it entertains me like the weather. Our eyes still stare and show that we care. Yes, our skin may be wrinkled a bit, but our souls won't ever quit. Getting older is a crown that no one should put down. We need to cherish these times, feeling good like nursery rhymes. When my eyes don't wake and my heart won't shake, I'll realize our life is through. What a sad revelation, but we'll end up at the same destination. As we say goodbye to the sun and moon, I know our souls will meet soon.

Not Forgotten

Been my spouse for so long, now you can't remember our favorite song. Love every line on your face, but you forgot how to tie your shoelace. It saddens me to see you transform; now this is your norm. Friends and family miss you so much; we're still willing to be your crutch. No one should be alone in the dark; I'll protect you like Noah's ark. Our grandchildren adore your smile; they like chasing you for miles. I bet God is not done with you yet. Nevertheless, you still know what's right even if you forget my name tomorrow night.

Final Blow

The smile in your eye has faded; we shouldn't have dated. Vacations we had together, doomed like hurricane weather. Our home was a miraculous sight; now it's just a place where people say good night. Children's toys are packed in a basket while our marriage is buried in a casket. You can say goodbye to us; we choked on trust. Lawyers have arrived at last to erase our disgraceful past. The judge is ready to strike; he doesn't care who we like. Remind me who wins so we can add that to our sins. Like a puzzle, we must figure out our trouble. Being alone is what you desire, kicked me out like an umpire. I'll leave you with this thought: don't forget you were bought. Keep believing you're better than I; bad news, we ended in a tie.

Goodbye

Staring at the beautiful lawn is a treat, except for what lies beneath. You promised I would never be alone, but now you have another home. We prayed this would happen much later, changed by God who is greater. Don't want to be alone, you'll never call my phone. No one should see me cry, especially you who wasn't supposed to say goodbye. Our children won't be the same; they refuse to say your name. The hurt we share is too much to bear. Thought about joining you in the hole, but then our story wouldn't be told. You promised not to die first, now I'm cursed.

About the Author

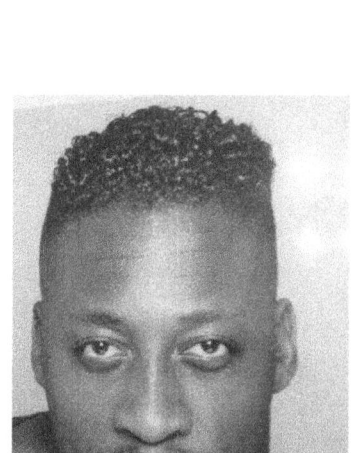

Michael G. Wright was proud to be born in Jamaica and grow up in America. After graduating from Southern Connecticut State University with a degree in bachelor of science in journalism and minor in communications, he worked as a reporter for the *Hartford Courant* and *Meriden Record-Journal*. During that time, he was also a linebacker for the Hartford Mustangs, a semiprofessional football team. He also managed nightclubs and owned Uptown Upscale Lounge. Furthermore, Michael acted in independent movies and ESPN commercials. Also, he competed in mixed martial arts competitions and coached high school wrestling.